Songs for the Cleveland Avenue Warriors

Poems from the past, present, and future

by Gary E. Moore

Published by creativeonion Press in Michigan, 2021

Editing & book design by Marjorie Steele
Cover art by Melolagnia

Copyright creativeonion Press, all rights reserved.

Any similarity between any of the names, characters, persons, events, or institutions in this publication to actual names, characters, and persons, whether living or dead, is untintended and purely coincidental.

ISBN 978-1-7345816-4-5

ISBN: 978-1-7345816-4-5

TABLE OF CONTENTS
Songs for the Cleveland Avenue Warriors

Book 1: An assortment of lamentations for the dead   7
Songs for the cleveland avenue warriors   8
Monsters moved about at night   18
The inherent paradox of ascension   19
Gordan parks, renaissance man   20
Playing chess with dragons   21
And houses burn   22
Back in the day   23
A middle aged cup of coffee   24
Spliffs and long sips from plastic cups   26
Like a blues song   28
Fifty shades of black   29

Book 2: Seasonings   *31*
I used to be a superhero   32
The weather   34
Zavy goes back to school   35
Slow burning fall leaves   36
Ready for some football   37
Independence   38
The slow burn of decay   39
Fall: a season of change   40
Gone is emptiness   41
Snow days   42
School days now   43
Crumbling herb   44
Thanksgiving   45
Fall   46
Potheads   47
Lightning rods   48
High school stars   49
Amalgamated man   50
The creation, version one   52
The creation, version two   53
The creation, version three   54
Let's talk awhile   55

Copland 56
Recorder of will chronicler of dreams 57
A sudden congregation of birds 58
Waiting for the bus 60
Sol 61
Drip and drizzle 62
Compost 63
A decatur street holiday celebration 64

Book 3: Subversion   67
Burt's bees 68
High times for high society 70
New york big city of dreams 71
Good citizens love the police 73
Untitled 74
The truth of a love 76
Delroy lindo 77
What daddy do 79
Fire drills 80
I can't even watch tv in peace 81
Supernatural levitation 82
Mother wolf 83
Lost 84
I trust no one 85
Conspicuous consumption of cocaine and capitalism ... 86
Holy man 88
Corporate christianity 90
Revolutionary rebirth 91
My third world friend 93
Welcome to the fair 94
God's face 95
Shopping trips 97
Adolescent innocence 98
Henrietta lacks 99
A fine meal 101
Seeking substance 102
Petit mort 103
The rising cost of concession 105
Times they are a-changin 106

Sometimes the world don't make no cents	107
Historical archaeology	108
Lost	109
Oh my	110
I want to go back to wrigleyville	111
Quarantine	113
Untitled	114
This world ain't made for lovers	116
Spent shells and sea shells	118
Success looms	119

About the author — *120*

"...no time of starched and ironed innocence. Godfearing elders, even Godless grifters, tried as best they could to shelter us. Rats fighting in their walls."

Robert Hayden, Elegies for Paradise Valley, 1975

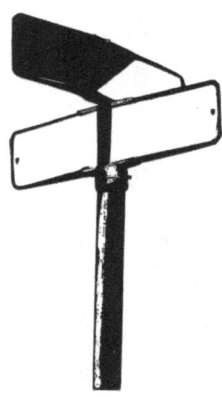

**Book 1:
AN ASSORTMENT
OF LAMENTATIONS
FOR THE DEAD**

SONGS FOR THE CLEVELAND AVENUE WARRIORS

I

Childhood was fun in shifts; a great play
with no script; a short-lived haiku;
brick dust and mysteries; crushed glass
and vanities. It was children running

about to see with blind, unseeing eyes.
Tripping over the winos who we knew
by name and named for tragedy.
We knew where the dope houses were

and the burned out cars, where the hookers dipped
out of sight with greasy-palmed tricks
and the best places to go and hide
and blush and try to catch a glimpse.

So very different from waiting outside
in the rain while Mama worked upstairs
to pay rent, or for simply enough to feed
her howling children's many shifting needs.

Us kids seemed to take it all in stride,
blinded by the follies of youthful pride
and obligated to defend her honor;
"I bet y'all would fall over yourselves

to tend to me if I didn't care
or let you starve like the Clark family,
who don't eat if the boyfriend's run out
of beer!" No! No! No, Mother! Untrue!

We've been scouring the neighborhood
in search of gold! In search of flowers!

In search of treasure to bring to you!

       II
They tell me you left
soon after me,
seeking the same
differences, something new,
more adventure and
nightclubs that close at three.

I tried college at first.

It didn't work.

And the army couldn't overlook
the trials of my tested youth.

I found love and reefer,
loss and pain,
the trick to hiding hurts
and using tragedy
to serve my purpose.

I learned to embrace deceit
and to use the tools
of past defeats.

And you?

Are these the things you've learned, too?
Or were my lessons unique to me,
to be felt but not shared;
heard but unseen?

Either way,
I don't wish that you
too know my pain,
but wouldn't that be

a pretty strange
and coincidental thing?

      III
Such happy fools were we,
dancing madly
beneath the strobe light
of nuclear Armageddon.
Cutting a rug
in dirty pools
of a sickly yellowed
street lamps' glow
while bullets flew
and angry men
cut through the din
of anarchy and rebellion,
intent on securing
our consumer's hearts
and stamping out
 forbidden desires
and indignant demands
for rights,
for peace,
for no more than fun,
with rattled sabers
and drawn guns.

      IV
Oh how we can just
simply live amidst
the stench of tragedy.

This skill was taught to us
at the breast and fed
to our infant minds
like cautions against

hot stoves and broken glass,
the edges of coffee tables
and a healthy fear
of the police.

All throughout,
our innocence sloughs away,
dead skin, useless
to the burgeoning
chrysalis.

But, Time, irrespective of
mortal considerations,
maternal Empress of
a newborn's sense
of longing, rocks
the child to sleep beneath
false impressions
of adulthood,
secreting away

the truth of aging's
consequence.

       V
She smelled like a psalm,
A-framed like a
designer's dress.

Her hair was black
and slick with
Dark & Lovely, coconut-
scented and
beautifully glowing.

Not many girls from round
this way could
afford a weekly

straightening comb,
let alone
a sew-in or some box braids.

But she kept the
cantcha-dontchas
out of her kitchen
and tossed back silken
bangs without pause,

flicking her hair
aside, brushing back
stray locks like
the valley girls
on the cheerleading
squad.

Her angelic eyes
and cherubic nose
kept thoughts warm
through long summer
seasons and cold
winter nights
with a passion
that would erupt
in spring,

victim to a boy's folly
and the effects
of such during
the vernal months.

Shaken up though,
early on in March,
the deadly Ides
still turned to greet
their Emperor
with wicked and
lascivious delight.

And while most all quiet,
withdrawn boys
harbor a secret place
within their hearts
for some lost or
forbidden or fictional love;
the ball player's date,
prom queen to
some Adonal King;

years removed

after all the pretty boys
have fallen away,
they can sometimes
catch themselves
the dream girl,
resplendent in her
coat of many years,

if not just slightly worn.

    VI
You can't find a hooker's haunts out past
the 'woods or the longview housing projects.
Painted ladies calling illicitly
to the neighborhood boys, promising

delight and adult fantasy.
Rubbing their index fingers
under the noses of those bold enough
to venture close. 'You like that?' they'd ask,

cackling and crying out over rouged
shoulders to weary-eyed associates,
'Yeah, girl! This one here, he almost ready!'
What better lesson is there to learn?

When poverty extends its super
fluous form into many small and
mundane places, it teaches children
in different ways than does suburban

educations.

VII
There was a familiar face in the papers;
listed only as John Doe, Deceased.
Someone perhaps from the old neighborhood.

Remembered as a long-head fellow, dressed
kind of shabbily, no different than most
of the residents from that side of town.

We still knew the trick of hanging cool
from our waists like counted coup, though;
dragon's teeth to accentuate the frayed
fringes that are haute couture now, but were
symbolized through necessity then.

He got shot in the ass with a bb gun
two weeks from the start of our
freshman year. He lived to tell that tale
and many others, lurid stories of
dependence and addictions, ups and downs,
beginnings and ends to beat the band.

But what would he say at his own
bereavement? Would his sad, sunken
eyes draw the crowd to the edge of
their seats? Could the crushed and beaten
mouth evoke exclamations from them all?

I hadn't heard his name in years. Years?
Who am I kidding? More than two decades
now separated me from such turbulent

innocence. I was a fool, rushing
wildly towards the sound of a gunshot.
In search of another scrap to add
to my book of adolescence.

Troy. I'm sure that was his name.
I can only guess that he too
made it to adulthood, if only
to die unnamed, a gaunt-faced John Doe
in the on-line obituaries of my local,
Sunday morning paper.

VIII

Remember Mike, the kid with the limp?
Stuttering Steve or Sid the Gimp?
Our strongman, Bruno, what happened to him,
Or Lying Lamar, who served five to ten?
Is there anyone of you that knows,
anyone of you who has seen?
Where is tight-pants Betty, bright-skinned Irma Jean?

Remember Spin-Around, the Screaming Drunk,
twirling madly in the streets till she dropped?
What happened to Big Al, basketball god?
Does he still work over at the steelyards?
Is there anyone of you that knows,
anyone of you who has seen?
What of cousin Dennis, the Dancing Machine?

What happened to Fred, tough Fred who shot Joe?
Shouldn't he be out on parole?
Where is Marcus, the ladies' man,
Rico the DJ or the preacher's son, Sam?
Is there anyone of you that knows,
anyone of you who has seen?
Where is Big Juanita, who stood six foot three?

Are any of the Warriors still here?

Top or Bobby, raising toasts of warm beer?
Can you remember how they used to fight,
with fists and clubs and raised voices at night?
Is there anyone of you that knows,
anyone left behind who's seen, just where
these secrets were buried beneath the streets?

IX
you little black boys
need to learn.
you need to learn
how to run.

you little black boys
need to learn
how to run.

soon enough you'll learn,
if you ever plan
to live very long,

that you will need
to know
how to run.

for every
little black boy
that did live long,
rest assured,
he learned
soon enough,
how to run.

X
Incense burns in backrooms of beauty shops
and on storefront altars all lain with wreaths

to commemorate the dead; young and old,
the long gone and the recently deceased.

MONSTERS MOVED ABOUT AT NIGHT

monsters moved about at night
with guns and knives
and loose morality.
their filthy love and exuberance
forever staining the streets
and marking the darkness
with shouts
of disbelief.

THE INHERENT PARADOX OF ASCENSION

The streets were watching while I made my
ascent, casting dispersion and regrets,
leaving little room for variation so
that my own justifications rung hollow
upon my brother's ears. His illusions
promulgated for maintenance's sake.
And if my brother, then what of my friends?
I'm beholden, just like them, if not much
less, to an over-riding faith in man's
institutions. It just seemed to be
that I saw the strings. I peeked behind
the curtain. Threw back the covers
and saw the reality. And what's most
interesting, the less I pretended,
stood alone, refused to bend, the higher
I ascended. Both spiritually
and mentally. In my maturity
and financially. But what do I say
to James? A brother for more than just
a brother's sake. Who ran with me
and more than once shouldered the blame?
A trusted friend, hell-bent nonetheless
on self-destructive interests.
Who refused to change for love of same.

What do I say to James?

GORDAN PARKS, RENAISSANCE MAN

Trouble seemed to hound a man
throughout the seventies and eighties
and deep into the new millennium.
Joys matched up with pain and life with death
and time suffered reprieve for none.
Least of all the wretched of the Earth.
Some, then, chose capitalism
over their fading revolutions.
Prosperity in exchange for valuation.
Strange, perhaps, but not beyond wonder
in this land where warriors fight their battles
over two-hundred and fifty dollar meals
and a fine Chianti or Merlot.
Our leaders no longer snap necks
and suck marrow from the bones
of enemies vanquished in righteousness.
This way, now, is much more acceptable
to the scions of influence,
the children of the damned, set loose upon
the innocence of small town farm boys
and the naive visionaries caught like flies
on the pins of historic introspection;
fading snapshots, forgotten biographies
and rescued third world boys left behind
to trumpet the tales of the victor.

PLAYING CHESS WITH DRAGONS

It's not that any of us
actually wanted to be here.
Though some did seem unusually
complacent in regards to the surroundings.
But to sit in the county jail day room
when the new games arrived seemed a bit like
Christmas. A chess and checker set
eliciting ooh's and ahh's
from world hardened convicts, rapists, dealers.
And once the gaming began in earnest,
the activity loosened their tongues
and forged new ties amongst strangers
linked only through the fraternity
of societal criminality.

I sat and smacked bones, threw cards, played chess.
Talked loud and aggressively. Fit right in.
Became a brother to dragons and beasts.

Until, that is, I admitted my crime:
driving on a suspended license.

"Checkmate!" I cried delightedly,
to a room now filled
with suspicious
silence.

AND HOUSES BURN

--and houses burn while thirteen year old boys
cry in the night like lost children, leaving
most all to wonder at the cause for this,
by who's decree have we descended
into the depths of such despair?
Such despondency and confusion?
Are the staccato rhythms of gunshots,
the squeal of tires and the terrified
screams in the night to be
our fiery conclusion?
A blood-soaked crescendo which swells and swells
until all is consumed within
its corridor of sound, a wailing
cacophony awash with the songs
of urbanity. Turning tragic
consequence into the commonplace.
There is no more decency left
in the decisions made which
rule the lives of the lost; proudly wearing
tough exteriors that barely serve
to hide the hurt little boys inside.

BACK IN THE DAY

Ya'll remember draggin round a cardboard
box and your boom box and tucking pant legs
into socks so they could flash while your legs
would whirl and spin in dynamic circles
among hard-clapping friends who kept up
the pace and stomped out the beat while beat-
boxing and shuffling feet, tapping out
a mad rhythm on playground picnic
tables beneath graffiti-bombed
pavilions surrounded by stretches
of sun-scorched grass--?

Back when vacations meant squeezing into
the back of wood-paneled station wagons
and packing paper bags filled with fried
chicken and heading off
to the funeral for some long distant
uncle or aunt or great-great grand
on either parent's family's side
who stayed to hold thangs down, down south,
where black folks rushed to get out
in a great migratory wave that
recedes now back to whence they came.

I remember when it was ok.

When first cousins were expected
to be best friends because of mama 'nem
and the ties that bind and bound us back
to keep our safety nets in tact
were welcomed and loved and adored
for all the meaning, the love, the life,
the gifts and prayers we're now left here with,
alone, imploring--

A MIDDLE AGED CUP OF COFFEE

We sit and sip from chipped coffee cups
and lament the souls we lost through time.
We laugh at all the times we had and look
for love in the times gone past. So strange,
at this age, to consider what's served
to anchor certain memories. Dreams
of what was for me, what is, and what will
soon be, converging in early morning
as I mourn with a fellow traveler
along these lines. Trying to discern
the intent behind such intricate
designs which deign to reveal themselves
only in millennial arcs that bend
well out beyond our sight.
This is the best we've settled upon
as we concede to the erosion
wrought upon anyone who walks
through an age of reason, leaving us
searching for a reason in the scattered
ashes of what passes for the rapidly
advancing seasons. There was so much,
too much to worry for; what we've seen
and done and left undone. And midway
through this age, we've left behind the rage,
the regrets and the chaotic thoughts,
so filled with disarray, and look deep
into the calm containment within
a coffee cup and consider what more
is left to come and if someone should chose
to come along one day and wonder
what it was that we once found
so wonderous, as they sit and sip
and stare down into the depths

of their own well-worn
and cracked coffee cup–

SPLIFFS AND LONG SIPS FROM PLASTIC CUPS

I sure do miss firing up a spliff
and taking a sip of jack
from a CC Club cup clicking with cracked
ice cubes while shooting cues in musty rooms.
I miss the muse, the 4am rendezvous
when we'd meet and drink and think and creep
through the streets after 3rd shift clocked out
to eat and congregate and relate
their latest escapades. Those were the days.
We'd grown to know who we'd become and come
into ourselves even when the certainty
sent off sparks. Stone tempering stone.
I couldn't stand that dude sometimes
and at times was blind to just how much time
was gone before it counted. But since
he was here, I've learned of fear. Not the kind
that came from clinging to your big brother's
back as he hurled you downhill on the back
of a bike with no brakes, wild laughter,
like the whipping wind, streaming across
your face, but fear. Of life. Of love. Of death
and dirt and mud and closed caskets
and ashes and being forgotten
when time can no longer be extended.
Relevance in the face of infinity
is a dream. But dreams shape the boundaries
of our reality, and when we dream
collectively, we extend the reach
of our possibility. I dream
of a dude in a ratty house coat,
cussing and puffing on an ever
present blunt while bluntly dissecting
what's least expected, calling attention
to what would normally go unmentioned.

I miss the discussion. The challenge.
The slow sips from plastic cups pilfered
from a pool hall filled with smoke and spilled beer.
Little moments filled with such portent
in hindsight represents a fulfillment.
This is what it means to live. To be
something more, to be relevant.
A small town knockabout spouting off
about religion, politics, love
and esoterically musing over death
and it's unexplored opportunities
is the height of life and what's left
when all else has been stripped.
What audacity; to be missed. To have lived
as if it were a gift. To leave behind
a solemn soul sipping wine, simply
wondering about all of it--

LIKE A BLUES SONG

I mourn in the dark,
alone,
like a blues song,
listening to the tick
of time and
creaking wood;
the sounds of absence
where laughter once bloomed
in lieu of the hurt
and anger and the
misunderstanding
wrought from my penchant
to sit with regret
and loss as I mourn,
alone,
in the dark;
like the blues song.

FIFTY SHADES OF BLACK

Back when I grew up
black had no nuance.
It either was or it wasn't.
There were no shades of gray
on South Side streets
that reeked of the spoiled dregs
of beer that ran
in rivulets across
cracked concrete
while desperate mothers
tried hard to keep their kids
from hearing them weep.

Black either was or it wasn't.
As armor. As necessity. As need.
It wasn't allowed to talk white
on Mueller Park playgrounds
while the DJ's got lit
and the block parties went down
and it dare not speak outside the lines,
to explore more than
what was best to keep
me fed at sixteen and
lost out on the streets.

Black kept those dreams and
romantic idylls to a minimum
in the company of killers,
drug dealers, Cadillac driving pimps
and Chamber of Commerce bound politicians.
It was wary of who listened,
of who may have chosen to strike from spite,
uncertainty, or misunderstanding,

cause black was or it wasn't.
At least, it was, for whom it was
most important. And,
the police, and our teachers never seemed
to see the difference, and they each
enforced their law with extreme prejudice.

**Book 2:
SEASONINGS**

I USED TO BE A SUPERHERO

I used to be a Superhero.
Or at least I'd pretend to be.
You know. The kind in tights and real cool shades
and a big cape that rippled and flowed
around my body. I was hard as stone
and immovable. Looking out from atop
The Citizen's Bank Building, staring
wistfully like the seldom seen hawks
that used to frequent this place, I'd search
the city below, my city, for crimes
against the poor folk that I knew
would find no help in Superman
or Batman. Hell, even the Black Panther
seemed to be too busy saving
the Universe to save the victims
of my Old King's Orchard neighborhood.

Or a good friend, shot dead long ago
on an unseasonably cold
April Fool's Day.

I looked quite a bit like Dr. J,
with a real big afro and some bad ass
Chuck Taylor's on to match my cape.
I wore red boxing trunks and floated,
like a winged insect
alight upon a gentle breeze,
and yet my powerful blows, made mighty
in Justice's name, rang out and stung
like some deadly barbed beast.

I dreamed of superpower and salvation
as a child and searched, as I grew
to become a man, for the means

to be a Superhero.

THE WEATHER

I don't much mind
rainy days.
These are just the
spring time blues
walking round
in a Central Illinoisan's
shoes. Grey skies
swoop and sway
like hawks adrift
in search of prey
and lines of storm
break fast like
crashing glass and,
suddenly still, the
air feels pure. Crystal
clear and certain
and sure. These are the
times to be inside.
To huddle close with
little feet in need of
comfort when the
thunder shakes the eaves
and rattles teeth.
We live with rain.
Rejoice for and regret
its arrival and overstay
and express our time
worn platitudes;
just wait, the weather's
sure to change today.

ZAVY GOES BACK TO SCHOOL
(gone, gone, good times gone)

September seems so far away in June.
Firelight nights, warm, wet, like the hot breath of
God smiling down on quick youth,
the quickened breath and the thudding heartbeat
of fast feet slap slapping against concrete
heated, enticing, in the midday sun.
A race track, a track lane, an adventure's
early beginning. Each step forged in flames
fanned high by an idle complacency
that crept into initial excitement
over hard fought freedoms won in winter,
fallen prey to the appearance of gold,
blissfully ignorant of gilded lead.
Time's great chasm calling forth to fleeting youth,
school bell's ring ring faintly in the distance,
barely heard above the din of baseball
games, laughter and splashing, cool pool waters.
All seeds sown in hearts and minds back in spring
bear fruit over the course of long hot days,
their bounty flush with possibility
and remorse for all the fruit left afield.

SLOW BURNING FALL LEAVES

We suffer slow burns. Simmering angers.
The dregs of our defeat, like the fall leaves,
left scattered round the base
of the desolate trees that grow
from the grates of neglected streetscapes.
Our lives are lived as lonely as these trees,
serving winehead bids for petty offenses,
blown about, wandering, aimless.
Just long enough, those couple of months,
for disconnection from our seed,
left spent, spun out on the swirling winds
that stir the leaves and leave behind
the running vines that can't wait for careful
cultivation. This is how a choking
weed, a willow's wisp, then overwhelms
with the pretty blooms that kill the innocent
belief in the allure of faerie mounds
and the Native cities that once rose above
the plains, before the trees were stripped away.
Their rooted memories, though, steeped into
the earth, still linger. Simmering.
A slow burn. A mycelial decay.
An essence, stripped away one ionic
layer at a time, so that
even a fleeting smile is preserved,
like amber, for future fools
to discover and declare it to be
the perfect representation
of this particular genus of trees;
despite the fact that it was destined
to live long and to die lonely,
surrounded by such great stretches
of concrete.

READY FOR SOME FOOTBALL

Feeling some type of way about the football games.
Kinda like watching a Mel Gibson flick
or a Mayweather fight or listening
to a Rick Ross song. You know, this shit
is cool, but, that dude will roofy you.
But the overall cultural paradigm,
as a stereotypically overt
overlay is filled with negativity
and an ouroboros-like penchant
for self-ingestion. We eat our young
as a sacrifice to the corporate
gods of consumption. 200 dollar
shoes are traded in for the lives of our
sons and daughters while we dream
of delivering them one day
to the NFL or the NBA
where together they are to cash checks
and forget, like a real American.
Standing proudly, saluting, as the flag
reminds that they can now participate.
They've been granted access to the club
on a preliminary level.
But how? Did they shed the skin? The shame?
The memories or recurrent moments
and fallen family? They are supposed
to brush off their own insistent
evidence of the guns in their faces,
the demeaning memes and a shut up
and play ideology, just accept
this gift of exclusion, offered up
to the few. Take the cake and eat it,
we say. They are no longer just black,
they've graduated, like OJ.

INDEPENDENCE

My Independence Day convo
with the kids begins;

"What kind of party ends at 12:30?
They musta been shootin?"

"I ain't even gon lie--"

"Yeah--"

"Man, that shit was crazy--"

No nicks no bangs no bumps no bruises?
Thank you, Lord, for your conclusions.
My life his life their lives/illusions.
Brief stays along a midge fly's
life, zipping in and out
without much left behind but
the shock and hurt and disbelief
that steeps and deepens
and grows in timbre while
a muzzle flash blasts away
at common sense, and bleary eyes,
squinting through blue smoke as a party
dissolves into chaos,
frantically search for the most
expeditious means of escape.

THE SLOW BURN OF DECAY

these lives,
these times,
are ruinous;
epistles
to a declining era.
a story told
through weathered rings
in ancient stone
strewn along the banks
of long dead rivers.
the receding waters
of familiarity
leaving a metallic tang
upon the tongue, like
licking a battery,
an anodal anointing
burning down the
buildings,
the blocks,
the memory of
all that defined
meaning,
reduced to ash
beneath
a tractor's wheel.
dissolution
becomes
us.

FALL: A SEASON OF CHANGE

I'm processing probabilities
faster than I can possibly explain
in the midst of a seasonal change.
Its time winding down,
its animus withdrawn,
now is when
conflicts will resolve,
their conclusions determined
amidst this shifting
uncertainty,
and the layers of depth and color,
which underlays it all,
will finally be revealed.
The Earth, stripped bare
following a harvest
of its fecundity,
will likely grow fallow
amidst the coming frost,
and yet hope resides
within the latent potential
of a single seed,
a genomic remnant
of past majesty,
set aside and dried and saved
for sowing, for when the earth begins
to warm again
and the current season,
once more, shifts and strains
towards another change.

GONE IS EMPTINESS

Gone is emptiness,
a vacuum given over to absence.
It's a distant echo
where your laughter used to be,
a fallow field, its color faded,
passed away into memory;
the fleeting thought of an alluring smile
that once brightened the dark despondence
that has now been replaced with malaise;
a wandering, restless pace
drummed into the thump-thump-thumping
feet that walk and walk and
seek and seek the cause of
such incongruity. The guilt, the
shame, the bruises, lies and blame,
all tangled about these restless
feet. Stepped across and trod upon
and soon enough forgotten,
left alone to distraction until too late,
a once stable presence ebbs, abates,
dissipates into an elusive fog that
slips so quietly away.

There is no good means to supplant
this swift sense of decay, once set
upon its course, though from such
reminiscence and remorse perhaps
a new thing grows. Long cold
seasons tend to determine such things
as the cold dry air burns and scalds away
the possibilities, the need, for redress,
and the empty spaces begin to echo
less and less.

SNOW DAYS

A gray day overlays last night's
plain sights and scenes and dreams of great tracts
of billowing grass and fluff-filled breezes
drifting past as silent snowflakes break
the spell of far off prophecies that
foretell of morning suns which ignite
whole fields filled with fog and reflective drops
of dewy dawn, conjured up on the last gasp of winter's
dying breath. The truth of self, all that's left
when drifts piled high along the sides of roads
and walkways and paths to nowhere
begins to disappear, receding
beneath the ceaseless beat of warmer days,
still yet to come, calling to our conscious
need, a dormant seed, is viable still
beneath the frozen soil that slowly ticks
and slips and warms beneath the same sun
that reigns over these last snow-filled days.

SCHOOL DAYS NOW

So sad. Such harm. Hidden behind quick smiles
and charm and tipped desks and voices raised
shrilly in distress. Listen closer up
though and the body language changes.
It speaks more truth than mere words can convey.

We can't even come to the park to play,
they say, so why must I sit and raise
my hand when nothing dreamed is guaranteed?

I'm lost. We're done. I have no sense
of being anywhere, for any reason,
when it all slips away, caught on the edge
of a sand-sucking hole as my feet
scrabble and kick and search for purchase
amidst the shifting elements.

Childhood ain't supposed to be this way,
the rest of us say. As if things had changed
for the working poor since the dawn
of the industrial age.

CRUMBLING HERB

You smell that? he said while crumbling herb
upon a plate of fine China.
That's the smell of earth, sky and wilderness.
It's the smell of nature, rainy days
and your grandmother's root cellar.
This is the scent that rolls across the moon.
Sinks down into your basement. Lives there,
in the fresh spring dirt, burrowed through with worms.

Not bad, his captive audience replied,
looking about in admiration
at the horticulturalist's
impressive collection
of universally good graces.

Not bad at all.

THANKSGIVING

Black folk scattered like leaves
fallen from a Southern tree.
Haplessly thrown to the wind
and left to settle where they may,
families would split and shift
across the continent and find root,
seeding the land they and their forebears
helped to cultivate with blood
and steel and cracking whip.
There are no small miracles then
in their gatherings,
the drawing close of distant kin,
and wondrous reunions erupt in haste
to celebrate their thanksgivings.

FALL

Perhaps it is that time of year.
When desperation sets in,
like the fall seasons,
and I lose favor for all my passions;
my art, my work, my love.

You see, the harvest months are hardest
on a blackman in America.
It's as if primal instincts, born in warmer
climates, still tug at fading soul-strings.

And this is so much worse.
This hungering in the cold,
shivering with no hope for heat,
more indomitable.

The autumn winds foretell of the fallow Earth.
The time when God fulfills his promise,
withdrawing his breath from growing things
and offering up no reprieve.

POTHEADS

They smoke like kings come harvest.
The reefer cigarettes as big around
as your finger.

By late fall they roll
no more than pin joints
and have nothing but the greasy stains
left behind in pipes and bowls
in deep winter.

Come spring, they prepare
the earth for a new season
and resow their garden.

LIGHTNING RODS

their bodies, slick
with the pounding rain,
writhed and screamed and
squealed in delight as
they danced in the storm.
a ten pm hair-raiser, it grew
and spread, not like a disease,
but a cure, across the landscape.
the lightning lit the air and thunder
ripped wide the black of night
while their mother, and some
vaguely familiar friend or 'uncle',
sat inside and cursed
the flickering tv screen.

they were happy little lightning rods.

HIGH SCHOOL STARS

He soared like a bird caught on a current
as it rose to its perch.
His home, as high as an aviary,
sat atop the Cassel Court Apartments,
not far adjacent from John's Hill Park,
right in the center of playground decay;
broken bottles and millions of minute
splinters of glass that kept the kids and
the stragglers off the court until he came.

Summertime on the Hill brought treats for all
who dared the blistering heat rising in
waves from the baking spot of cracked asphalt
that hosted a fallen angel these days.
Old King's Orchard's saving grace, salvation
in mid-tops and a mesh jersey.
Heralded in the big city, coddled
at home and school and in life until
the real world closed its teeth across his will
and ripped away his confidence.

Throughout the week the Hill hosted stars
and angels and gods. Now, earthbound,
left behind to weep and to play.

AMALGAMATED MAN

I am colored like an ashen dawn
and sprout cotton from atop my head.
Dirt, black and rich, crumbles between my toes
and pure, clean water, a river's worth
of salutation, filled with fishes
and exotic life, flows from my heart.

Bearing the crest of my many colors,
the greens and golds, the reds, yellows, blues:
electric blue, indigo, cerulean--
a rainbow unfurls about my hips,
bleeding out and staining the brittle parchments
inscribed with the secret equations
written down in God's secret language.

My mouth is a fount of eternity.
All things, great and small, real or indifferent,
great plumes of substance, spring from my loins.

My legs are tree trunks, my hands the branches.
My eyes are gaping holes of flame
as I peer into a volcano's throat
and match its primal scream with my own.

I am the panoramic view
of rolling meadows, soaring mountains
and fathomless oceans.
Dander falls from my scalp, whitening
the fields with snow.

I am Gabriel's trumpet. Angelic.
A living instrument of the green Earth,
my soul throbs with the pent up energies
that lie chambered within her core.

Here I am, an Amalgamated Man.
A living metaphor. My moods flashing
and shifting like the changing seasons
as I rotate slowly about God's glory,
cycling through the phases of the moon
and keping counsel with the sun
as I dance along the horizon.

THE CREATION, VERSION ONE

One day,
      Jesus wept
and the firmament ripped.
He batted his eyes
and the thunder crept
across the newly formed
earth and seas.
He brought the darkness
to its knees and then
He sought and toiled
and scratched and found
a place to sit
his tired ass down.
Later, still lonely
for more company
than just his left hand,
he reached down to where
his seed had struck the sand,
scooped it up along with the dirt
and shaped and formed
a black man.

THE CREATION, VERSION TWO

God sat one day
and took a toke
and stared into
the reefer smoke
and dreamed up suns
and moons and worlds
and soon got caught up
in the airy swirls.
He stopped to work it
out in his head,
starting out small at first,
he then decided on
a universe instead.
Having no one else to tell
of his great plan,
God went on
and created man.

THE CREATION, VERSION THREE

god winked
and his tv blinked.
he snapped his fingers
and out flowed rivers.
flipping through
the tv guide,
he changed channels
to see what
there was to find.
and right there,
between channels 9 and 10,
was a whole new reality
waiting for him to begin.

in need of an audience,
god then went on
and created us.

LET'S TALK AWHILE

let's talk awhile
in late December,
eat tacos and speak
with truculence;
tell tall tales
of dreams and love
and wanderlust
and find, perchance, some
means to dance and
to lose ourselves in
forbidden romance.
the more scandalous
the better.
the excitement
leading on to pleasure.
a delightfully carnal
incursion. we can dwell
upon the stars as the snow
softly falls. postulate
on the celestial ellipse
of bodies in motion
and contemplate our deaths
over bottles of fine wine
and political subversion.

COPLAND

Cruising on a hot, humid summer night,
I see cops crouched like sinners
in the corners, alleyways and sidestreets,
awaiting my passage, shadowing
my slow drag across the ballroom floor,
hiding and dodging and weaving
like Ali in a rope-a-dope,
and I'm still only looking for some weed.
Not Anthrax or gold-metal plated
Kryptonite spliced with wheat germ and freeze-dried
for easy distribution. Don't you know
that their reasoning, like their love,
their life and their politics, are no more
than illusion? Kinda like
the policeman's creed: "To Serve and Protect."
Everyone, that is, but me.

RECORDER OF WILL CHRONICLER OF DREAMS

Late night it seemed, early morning in fact.
The street lies low, giving up its secrets,
shadowy movements, cooling cars
and a late night argument
that spills from the one house still lit
against the black and moonless murk.
A somnolent obtrusiveness
drifting through solid walls. Such trouble,
such pain befalls the perpetual
inhabitants of uptown streets
and prejudiced visions of bar fights,
brothels and all night stores,
decadence and debauchery
their only wares.

Shrouded in cloud-black, blue-black night,
the heat of a summer's day slowly
drifting up and away as
I sit and smoke, watching, listening;
Recorder of Will, Chronicler of Dreams.
Curling hazy rings of forgotten things
about my head,
I should have learned from experience,
insomnia tends to breed
the oddest relationships,
and not all things are meant
to be seen.

A SUDDEN CONGREGATION OF BIRDS

A sudden congregation of birds
drew my eyes to the slate gray skies.
Wheeling and turning and dipping about
and rising on unseen currents,
tumultuous winds. Forces which can't
seem to dim the grace of the noisiest
of scavenger birds. Granted flight,
the desire for heaven stitched into
their energy-efficient little bodies,
I want to fly. To lose myself inside
the firmament. Leave this earth for life
amongst the clouds, bid gravity adieu
with all its ponderous heaviness.
The avian urge for flight
misplaced within me, somehow. The ghost
of some lost genetic trait leading to
 a natural state of spatial envy.
It doesn't matter nor minimize
my wishes. I still just want to fly.
Experience life untethered, free
of the responsibilities that chain
the feet to concrete; condense time
into tight little packages; hours,
minutes, years. The infinite abides
above our heads and I want to soar
through its current. Spread my wings and look down
upon an abandoned life while basking
in the bosom of eternity.
The simple dreams of an earth-bound being.
Wishing. Reaching. Falling further away
from a lifetime spent down upon the rock.
Forever searching the skies for like minds.
Feeling the pull of the winds against
our unfeathered skins. Dying with the weight

of heaven's denial.

WAITING FOR THE BUS

Passing cars show no mercy
to those waiting for the bus
while standing in the rain.
All they can do is stand
and drip and mope and hope
that soon the season changes.

Merciless, passing cars
that swoosh and zip by and spray.
Splashing and soaking soggy fortunes
on cold November days.

While moistened hair lays stiff
and rough cloth binds along the seams,
the rain turns the bus fare cold
inside heavy, burdened jeans.

Swift and sleek uncaring cars
that seem so warm and clean inside,
sliding along thin planes of rain
receding with the hope of being dry,
they never seem to slow at all
to ease the chilling waves.

SOL

I was pulled from deep within the land
of sand and extraordinary.
Gently stirred by Earth's slow rotation,
celestial and precisely balanced,
with softening horizons which announce
the inevitable. The world beneath
celebrates its awakening
with deep and resolute songs of dawning.
Calling forth approaching destinies
in spite of the imposed, daily cycles
soon to begin. Time cherishes each moment,
relishing each individual
awakening to the phoenix's rebirth.
A painless passing into the real world,
risen above such petty concerns
as poverty, cultural suppression
and envious plotting against
the love of her gifts.

The joy of beginnings withstands
tumultuous pressure from personal
gravity, sinking its tendrils into
this magnetic string of shimmering pearls,
pulled taut along silent chords, binding all
to the same harmonies which comfort
the sun on its morning sojourn
across the sky.

DRIP AND DRIZZLE

drip and drizzle.
drip and drizzle.
no outside today.
no bright sunshine
to brighten the kitchen
as it awakens
to a joyously raucous
mid-morning bustle.
maybe more fitting
for quiet contemplation
and slow sips of hot coffee
before padding feet
find their rhythm,
dragging a bit, at first,
then stomping and
demanding and
angst-filled and frightened.
and hungry. still, very
hungry; for food
and fulfillment and
security and comfort.
and less news. and
their friends. and
normality again.

it's ok, you'll say to them,
assuring yourself
as much as you can,
the rain will soon go away,
and the sun will come out
some other day.

COMPOST

I lit a slow-burning fire
in my backyard back in spring.
Its combustive, convective heat,
though, won't be apparent until deep
into the winter's sleep
as snow slides off the pyre
of decay that smolders and sinks
when atomic bonds are slowly released
and the fading chlorophyll contributes
to the fuel and flames
that will push back against
an icy earth and the hoary frost
which mists along the lowly places
and settles like a sigh
on slick surfaces.

I warm my thoughts across the rising waves
of this catalytic comfort, rubbing
my hands vigorously, stamping my feet,
imagining the warmth which wraps around
and soothes and caresses my face,
counteracting winter's sting
and the solstice's fast approaching,
cold embrace.

A DECATUR STREET HOLIDAY CELEBRATION

Huge brick houses line the streets,
built like guards against bad weather;
the winter storms and strong spring winds
that whipped across the plains
and challenged the intrepid
who came to seek their fortune
in a life or death struggle against
an unyielding sea of prairie grasses
and the natives, too secure
in their own place alongside nature
to recognize the threat
of an insidiously creeping,
burgeoning capitalism,
in search of gold, fur, exotic
spice and gems. Gilded and lit
with fire and ice while the holidays
raged and the debutante dances
debuted the daughters of industry
alongside a deep sense
of security, there was absolutely
no reason to think that the centuries'
progression would leave
these once celebrated cobblestone streets
behind, a row of once stately homes
now divided up into multi-unit
rental properties and drug dens
serving as a haven, the last resort
for single mothers and crying babies
and late payments come due
as the dirty snow accumulates
against the grates and curbs
and the empty bus stops
along abandoned bus routes

when winter settles in and
the disconnect notices are suspended
until spring and the current residents,
in some kind of macabre call back,
string up lights and delight
in a brief moment of respite,
and, in a wicked twist
to an homage to the past,
gather round and celebrate Christmas,
just like the founders used to do.

**Book 3:
SUBVERSION**

BURT'S BEES

Not even Burt can flirt
with that no nonsense,
live like what's best,
pass up the big cash,
sell just enough to get by
at some cutesy
little roadside stand.
Not many can just relax,
pay their taxes and live debt-free
on grandpappy's old family home
and feed the wood-fired stove
and hate and condemn
and debate the likes of the BLM
and the socialist dems
who sit by while the world
we'd known, the world
we have all become
accustomed to as
a matter of inevitability,
a once formidable, physical
property, like classical mechanics,
succumbs to the diminishing point
of singularity.

Burt got hurt and took
his worth;
some hippie's dream,
like Thomas Paine;

a couple acres of land,
a few bucks, young love.

Not much of value
to anyone with an eye

towards building empires.

Until the scope of potential
leaves scars and civil wars
and Jim Crow laws
that finally reduce the founders
to little more than dancing avatars;

or traveling memes
or caricatures printed up
and dispensed on myriad
product labels and embossed upon
the corporate literature.

HIGH TIMES FOR HIGH SOCIETY

I've seen conservatives snorting the
cocaine they'd brought with them in my kitchen
while a group of liberals smoked weed
in the dining room and complained about
the unfairness of their criminal
convictions, the unbalanced conditions.
Each of them had been stripped and frisked
and biased against on Fox and C-Span
and sentenced by the Supreme Court
of Upstanding Citizenship,
those who've deemed them less than men.
A Cosbian error, can't you see?
If you work hard you can be just as Oprah as me!
Join in while we advocate building
a wall across the border to keep out
The Brown Horde with no regard for the
repercussions of locking ourselves in.
Besides, what more is there to lose, other
than another generation of young
women and men? They are all steeped in sin,
so we won't miss them, right? They're just dealers,
so, even if they really exist
well below the averages lurking in
upper class comfort with political
protections, they look so guilty.
When they are gone, though, I recall
wondering that the exceptional
elite will still be passing out
at parties and their dealers will still tend
to look just like them. All the benefits
and none of the harassment. Exactly
as it was imagined.

NEW YORK BIG CITY OF DREAMS
(or: bboys changed my life)

New York from afar
was like a piece of art.
A living representation
of life adrift
amidst a conflict.
Two, to four to five
to a thousand
opposing points
of view, each askew
and a brand new
thing which exists
in part but never the whole
the whole world round
nor throughout the extent
and reach of history. And yet,
the New York that I knew
was featured on the
evening news. A bleak,
post-apocalyptic future city.
Crumbled tenements and tricks
and desperate times and
Times Square tales of stick up kids
and lost tourists. Seen from afar,
it was a cityscape draped in curtained
black against the backdrop
of rot and fecundity from which
would spring a song, a beat,
a dance which would speak
to me and more like me. A new
wave of social change like
butterfly collars and platform shoes,
smoke-filled rooms and slow
jazz tunes blaring right next
door to a country filled with

pretend club 54's .Way back when
cardboard dance floors became
a thing and b-boys recognized
themselves and learned
that they had a name from
East Coast slums to
Midwestern projects and all the way
out West. We were a people.
If New York knew, then it was true.
And so the whole world, too, they knew.
Because this was the Big City of Dreams.

GOOD CITIZENS LOVE THE POLICE

We seek.
We preach.
We pray for relief
and teach our kids
a healthy fear of the police.

Because good citizens, as defined
along racial, economic
and societal color lines,
shift the defense away
from the need for recompense.

Good citizens are accepting
of the paradigm and
teach their kids to fear
while sheltering behind
fresh kicks and designer gear,
gold chains and watches
and parties non-stop and
a wish list of 'ifs', 'maybes'
and lost opportunity.

Good citizens don't notice
the personal impact of POTUS
on generations of their own,
handicapped babies.

Even with their unique perspective
on the stresses of living tested. No.

We seek. We preach. We pray for relief
while we teach our kids
a healthy fear of the police.

UNTITLED

A natural rhythm is inherent
within the heartbeat of each atomic
entanglement. Each moment is pregnant
with the potential of song
and poetry exists within the midst
of even the most monstrous of what we
do for desire. Humanity swings
wildly to the tune of its darkest nature,
stirring the dust of forgotten needs in
the night as night-jars sing of predators
who hunt and seek to sink their teeth into
the warm, wet spurt of timpani, beating
wildly against the chance to defeat death
in a punctuated run of pounding
feet and wild cat shrieks; deadly melodic
revelries. Caged animals sing sweetly
as well. Their lament scouring the walls
of prison complexes. Man or beast or
yet most expediently defined as
political fodder, no one shall know
which voice cries out in sorrowful lament.
The difference is muffled by cement
and mortar and a cast iron doctrine.
These things realigning into a new
consideration for a symphonic
civilization. A rising, lilting
epic thing that crashes loudly about
the frightened souls held captive to a tune.
These are the damned, over trodden by a
drummer's marching feet, advancing progress
in metallic fits and starts and 3D
printed copies of how it all should sound
when the music ends and is replaced
by a sorrowful cry; a lone wolf's howl

punctuated by a deafening silence.

THE TRUTH OF A LOVE

The truth of love
is a
sharp edged, cruel thing.
A soulless blade,
slicing away, as
the physicality of this life retreats, a molecular
decay, and all succumbs
to inevitability; even the
Greatest of these Things
Fall Apart in millennia-long
arcs of continuity amidst
the sea of eternity.
The best that we can hope for
in all of this
is the chance
to say adieu to lost loves,
loved ones and dreams,
as life frays
at the seams and we decay,
and rot away,
beautifully into the mists
of a fleeting bit
of reminiscent love.

DELROY LINDO

Whatever lies beneath the
mask of indignation we are all
forced to don in lieu
of our own, discretely defined
identities, therein hides the truth.
What monsters lurk
beneath the smiles that
crack our granite
composure? None so
desperate as that which craves
definition from a
crowd-sourced complacency,
most certainly. Compassion speaks
with a forked tongue and
its proclamations are elusive
at best. A natural affinity
aligned with the nature
of the beast, I suppose. Oh, but here;
here is where the complexities
converge and shine, emit
their desire in a radiant bloom
of self-perfected majesty
that transcends the present day
amorphous definitions of beauty;
eroded, chiseled away from
black stone, its cracks
and crags and crevices
revealed in sweeping,
awe-inspiring architectural lines
built up high with
a most impressive grandiosity.
It's all set to crumble away,
fall off into the forgotten
myth of irrelevance, obscurity.

No matter at all to the incessant
march of most dismissive Eternity.
Still, to dream. To live. To love. These things
are created indelibly,
reside and define down beneath
the genetic limits of a fleeting,
flickering humanity.
This is where our art begins:
where beauty takes root,
quickens in the hearts and minds
of each who dare approach.

WHAT DADDY DO

I just did the dishes. Got dishpan hands.
But I did the dishes like a man.

I did a load of laundry.
Cleaned up my young son's smelly butt
and stepped on Lego blocks
and matched and mated all his socks.
And I did it all just like a man.

He likes noodles. I made him some noodles.
Campbell's Soup. Like my Moms used to do,
but I cooked his up like a man.

He cut his finger. Bled a bit.
My stomach flipped, but I ain't show it.
Just cleaned him up, put on a band-aid,
gave him some go-gurt, sent him back to play.
And I smiled after I did it.
I don't really know why, but, sometimes--

just watching him is enough and I forget
to remember to watch him like a man.
And then I can only see
how much I love this human being.
How much love he'll need--

From me. His Dad. Tasked with teaching
him how, while learning myself, to be a man.

FIRE DRILLS

Fire drills ain't just fire drills
when a look of pure panic flashes
across the faces of a group of
jaded juveniles as the alarm
first begins to sound. In that instant,
cold, uncaring adolescence reverts
to the truth; in spite of the practiced
postures and their disaffected natures,
they are still just vulnerable children.
Left in need, searching for safety,
security, they deserve guidance
from guardians who have no intention
of handing them a gun or teaching them
the benefits of the militaristic
and to duck and run and hide and panic
while their elected politicians
keep right on planning to pocket
the paper that rewrites the basic
recognition of what's right and what's wrong
with an easy acceptance of crying
kids cowering for cover in classrooms.

I CAN'T EVEN WATCH TV IN PEACE

My mind wanders past the pretentious
presentation and sneaks backstage
to poke about in the discard bins
and bothersome truths that are shredded
into minute bits of confetti
and soaked in the glutinous milieu
of pasteurization that renders all
that could even be slightly construed
as dangerous into something much more
easily recognizable in an
acceptable shade of homogeneous.
I just can't look past the punctuation.
The point within the exposition
that captures our attention and forces us
to stop and listen and never even
once consider the broadcaster's
true intentions before blindly buying
into what has been deemed
best as it pertains to a more
acceptable corporate state,
while being streamed across the net
and offered up as breaking news,
flashed in urgency
across everyone's tv screen.

SUPERNATURAL LEVITATION

Overcoming obstacles
while supernaturally predisposed,
my mind tends to overflow
with information overload.

A concrete jungle cry,
a primal scream,
an alibi,
I see through
God's unchanging eye
and find myself
in the mirror.

A distorted reflection
of what could be,
a dirty glass menagerie,
a raw-dog ass mentality.
Omnipotence. Tenacity.

I know why men
are harassing me
and forgive them
of their failure.
We often sit in judgment,
marking our time
by mocking the divine
out of a fear
for something greater.

MOTHER WOLF

I witness the end. The innocents
of an age left to fend for themselves
like wolves, wild pups, fighting for a place
amongst the teats. Sucklings weaned
on the rich Mother's Milk of corruption,
prejudice, and a bitter sense
of superiority.

Mother Wolf, why then do you cry?

Surely you must be swollen with pride,
bursting with the pleasure of creation.
You've loosed a wild bunch. A slavering,
righteous pack to bay at the waxing moon
and to act with swiftness as the arbiters
of your carnivorous code.

Flush with the satisfaction of the kill, they rampage,
yip and snarl and growl and snap,
over the ripened flesh of the vanquished;
bits of bone and viscera
caught in their teeth; a blood lust-filled mob
of innocents blindly following
their mother's teaching,

for she knows that
the whole world fears the carnivore
and that fear is power.

LOST

I'll have to find my own
way home. I just don't want to fight
no more. My feet are tired.
My mind ain't right and my back
is sore from lifting the flag
of promise that bears the
Crest of my Arms, the
harbinger of my Master's charms
and bangles and trinkets and shiny
privileges that serve to cover up
true intentions and political
motivations. What else would
the Kingdom of Capital export
but hungry entrepreneurs with
profit potentials dancing like
sugar plums through their
fat little heads and hands
ill-suited to fight for any
Texas oil-man's rights to get
rich and endow
some family name into
perpetuity. Old money doesn't
age until its born and
now's a good time to start
the screwing. We're still
adolescents, after all, in the youth
of our existence as compared
to Roman or Phoenician or
Aztec histories, so our hormones
run wild across the planet.
Unchecked by morality or compassion
or understanding or sympathy.

I TRUST NO ONE

You see,
I trust no one
when it comes
to the gun.
A stray bullet
may fly like
a fatal slip
of the tongue,
an accidental discharge
barked out
in an innocent
crowd of potential victims.
It all leaves my nerves
on edge. A high voltage
wire stretched tight
as I await the fate
of an itchy finger,
a tricky endeavor,
a nameless man
with lightning
quick hands
and an even faster
temper.

CONSPICUOUS CONSUMPTION OF COCAINE AND CAPITALISM

Conspicuous consumption,
capitalism, and an
overwhelming concern for the corrupt
conservatives copping cocaine
in the kitchen. Left to their own devices
they lose themselves amidst their vices
and deflect, or at least try their best,
the truth of their unfaithfulness.
This leads me to fear the right,
who flash fake smiles and prowl the night,
hiding behind their alibis,
a barely concealed contempt,
high tax brackets and religious lies.
Starting wars they don't intend to fight,
it pays to pray to the presidency,
reap the reward and live a good life,
lie to yourself, your children,
to your god, and to your wife.
And with only the godless as your enemy,
the poor man can go and fight overseas
and leave the spoils of war to those
who are white and worthy enough to earn
a buck and buy peace conservatively,
make a sacrifice of lesser men
to an unstoppable, undeniably
profitable, economic engine.
It all makes me want to leave off,
stopping only to pray
at the Temple of Microsoft,
check my spiritual balance
at First Bank and Trust, refreshing my soul
with Crispy Creme Donuts as I embark
on a journey across the southern

slave states, dodging my creditors
while in search of an elusive,
high yield annual percentage rate.

HOLY MAN

Must be losing my edge
as a holy man;
allowing the slow
encroachment of the easily
simplistic and dispelled
rumors, truths and
otherwise meaningless
exhibitions in minor keys
that tend to strike a
less sonorous note than
the melody of naivety
and the strength of
personal belief to creep
along the cement
and invade the spaces
meant for meditations on
tomorrow and the circumstances
behind my obligations
and denials, spiritual
tests and the roaring fires
left in the wake
of all my mistakes.

Reason escapes me
as I pray for a more
convincing truth,
and the wisdom to manuever
through the unknown,
and yet I can no longer
clear out the spiritual space
for contemplation
over the purpose
of my existence,
so the questions remain

and I am left alone
to explain the loss
of faith in my divinity.

CORPORATE CHRISTIANITY

Corporate concerns get caught
in the cocaine economies
hiding behind the curtains
of conservative Christian
condescension.
Such contradictions
collapse down around
our algorithmic morality
while homegrown terrorists
count the cost of poppies
grown overseas,
funding wars against
capitalistic interests
which tends to pay
its enemies handsomely,
co-opting the dead civilians
along with the remnants
of an obstinate insurgency.

Because a brown
and yellow man's economy,
born on the flat plains or hilly terrains
of a far off third world country,
could never compete
with a Madison Ave.
marketing strategy.

Besides, who would believe
that a mere beast
could arise from the East
to challenge our King James Authority.

REVOLUTIONARY REBIRTH

My mixed emotions, metamorphoses
and metabolism should not be
televised, but broadcast live
over wireless networks and gossip columns.
an online blogger's wet dream filled with
water, mixed drinks and marijuana,
I wish for a list of unconventional
travel tips to guide me to the next stop
along freedom's road to liberation,
but there is no room at the inn
to let me in, so I must sleep under stars,
cursing over finances and the cost
of operating an American car.
All the while bombs fall on midnight movie
reviews and I can see right through the hole
in my roof. I think they see me,
watch me as I watch tv, trying to dumb down
so as not to go insane, as if there
were no worse thing than crazy
in a mixed-up, money-driven society.
A whole culture teetering on the verge
of galactic lunacy. Samples of which
travel through the internet and come to rest
as examples on distant planets
so that whosoever picks up on this
transmission will maybe come seeking
evidence of an intelligence,
only to find it drained away
from poisoned rivers and lakes.
So while I wait, I check out the sky,
peering way out past the satellite's
voyeuristic eyes,
searching for the tell-tale signs
of my evolutionary intent,

and duck quickly beneath the shelter
of my tinfoil-lined tent.

MY THIRD WORLD FRIEND

Extending arms
and privileges
to the less fortunate
of the world,
we spread our love
like peaceful doves
in rocket-fired
symmetry.
We feed the needy
and infect them
with our greed
as we bless them
with our democracies
and voting rights
and SuperBowls
and intercontinental flights.

Welcome to you,
my third world friend!
My second one, too.
We righteously extend
our state of the art
arms and ordinance
in a warm group hug
to express our joy
at your subversion,
your suburban transformation,
your metamorphoses
into a prime vacation
destination.

WELCOME TO THE FAIR

Fair? Did you say fair?
Child, there is no such thing as fair.
That's a fantasy.
Like a sitting president's war;
Big Chief Dress-up
playing at make-believe.
It is a wish that can't exist.
Lobster tail and champagne
on LINC card budgets with no constraints.
A middle eastern war,
an all night store,
a street corner that never closes.
It is a child prostitution ring.
A dead Dr. King
and Ali the GOAT's words slurring.
Fair. You did say fair?
Such naivety.
What innocence you have
in the face of such realities,
but just to be fair,
I feel compelled to tell you,
despite the movie land fantasies,
there is no place left for you, my dear,
because that place just doesn't exist
outside of here.

GOD'S FACE

Sitting here drinking,
thinking about the cosmic comedies
that tend to play out religiously.
Whether true believer or atheist,
nothing can honestly step up and claim
dominion over any other modality,
quite truthfully, and yet the extremities,
at least to me, seem to serve the same god.
Hell, given the strength of their belief
or disbelief, it seems they both drive
Beamers, Hummers and Cadillac SUV's.
So, what am I to do, stuck in the middle?
Who's Holy Ass aren't I kissing?
If I can thank the Lord for such a fine
day, yesterday, for waking me up
and sending me on my way, isn't He
responsible for me sleeping late and
getting fired today? If Jesus is
the best thing, then Vishnu fucked up
monumentally. Mohammad is a
fraud and Odin died pointlessly upon
a sacrificial tree. So don't talk to
me unless willingly condemning me
and billions more to hell most
dispassionately. My Uncle was a
Muslim with no wish to hear me
pray over his corpse on Judgment Day,
and my Grandfather, the Baptist minister,
left me with words that made me wonder
if his beliefs were wrong like mine,
even though he seemed to live his life
philosophically. God has no face
and no time for games. And as a
universal ideology,

shouldn't everyone have the same
accessibility? Surely
Christianity tells us how to
function on a higher level of
exclusivity and the Muslims
and the Hindu see themselves as
elevated beings. And yet these beliefs
require condemnation and a certain,
limited means of seeing the complete
picture as presented. God doesn't fit
well with the small boxes used to package
up what consistently defies explanation.
Used as a ruse to gain admittance
to higher planes and eternal
justifications and cover-ups,
the power structures and by-products
of centuries of blind faith and trust
are the culprits of the weaponization
of religion.

SHOPPING TRIPS

Went to the mall
to check up on the war.
Got lost in sporting goods
and could not recall
what it was I'd come there for.
Found my way
to a public display
of protest marchers
with their placards
and their naive certainties.
Indignant, they were,
over the state of things
which were happening
at home and overseas.
Not our domestic or foreign policies,
but the alarming lack of
Christian fundamentals and democracies.
Turning away, my faith enslaved,
I took the escalator three flights up
to shop around for my morality,
Came away, instead,
with a brand new flat screen tv.

ADOLESCENT INNOCENCE

Red intentions, palpably deluding
good decisions, heart rate's intensity
blurring the edges of a tightly
defined reality. Much like a
looking-glass influenced perception
of what is wrong or right with the world
of adolescent expectations
and unrealistic dreams. Truth and
justice are narrowly interpreted
to fit an ever-shifting foundation
of liquid definitions, chemical
interventions flooding the addled
senses of those lost to senselessness.
Regrets are years away unless forced to
pay for unfortunate circumstance
and the statistical likelihood
of defeat at the hands of a world
which marks the path through time with cruelty.
Innocence remains the same, it just grew
up and changed its name to match the timbre
of the future, a discordant note
sounded from frustration recognizing
the sudden limitations imposed
by the constraints which bind the feet
and hands and tempers the desire
for spontaneous celebrations.

HENRIETTA LACKS

So this is how you died,
in whispers that you did not hear.
Left to an unheralded legacy,
a lingering immortality
that connects an advancement
to an atrocity,
modern day breakthroughs
pushed through by cutting edge scientists,
directly aligned with
the Tuskegee Experiments.

My darling,
a lab rat who loved to dance
with her kids and laugh
as if her life held meaning
beyond the meaningless value
placed upon such a simple thing
as consent in lieu of
entitlement.

So young. So bold. Burdened down
with the weight of everything that's wrong
with a coldly clinical eye
toward reciprocity,
explaining away the refusal
to correct a mistake
because of the hit
the stockholders may take,

capitalism clashes
with morality, leaving behind
the dusted remnants
of sharecroppers and a young mother
who loved to flash red nails

and strut in the midst
of an existential crisis.

No easy thing, to find recognition
as a human being,
in a society determined
to downplay such a thing.

A FINE MEAL
(going to war)

I watched my meal grow cold. Lost interest
in the fading wisps of steam that shrank
and dissipated like wilting orchids.
My appetite was gone. Turning even,
a disinterested eye toward
less appealing sights and smells;
death and chaos, madness at the gates
of a crumbling civility.
And not the finest of wines, Cabernet
or Sauvignon, could stir my prodigious
desire for fine food, exotic
aromas or the light clink of china service
wares against delicate crystal glasses.
I was struck by sudden melancholy
at my sister's grand announcement.
She was off to fight the war
and hadn't even asked
what I should think about it.

SEEKING SUBSTANCE

I seek substance. Less of the perceived,
the expected degree of success as
considered by the multitude,
emboldened by the cathode ray
which emits its instructions daily.
Such strange paths to walk when time seems to shift
beneath the feet of those out of step
with the commonly agreed upon
reality which covers everything
like a fine sheen of pixie dust
laced with the government's finest
mind-altering hallucinogen.

This ain't living. It is existence.
Less of a life, marked by being,
spirituality loses flavor
as the spoils of religion continue
to eat away at our moral
authority.

PETIT MORT

We all die a little
as we slip off into dream
and, just before dawn
we are to be reborn,
Atum, summoning the
Morning Star to rend
the darkness and splay wide
the myths, the monsters
that dine on innocence
in the receding shadows
that burn away, chased
and crazed through like
a dimly shattered glass
reflecting fleeting glimpses
of the sky's briefly
illuminating potential
as God smiles down
on Africa. On the African.
Even her distant offspring,
lost to an amorphous
definition of time,
a harsh dimension
removed from the
immaterial substance
of the dreamstate
from whence we came
to be beholden, caught like
wild dragonflies
suspended in millennia
old amber. We get choked
out now. Killed on
livestream feeds
while the world debates
the worth of a being

that once flew
and lived free amongst
the elements and had long ago
learned to abide
alongside the flow of eternity,
the griot extending our awareness
out across that never ending sea.
Here, now, we are encouraged
to go to sleep, checking
before drifting off,
for an algorithmic confirmation
of yet another man's death
by asphyxiation.

THE RISING COST OF CONCESSION

Voting rights were earned
through blood and yet
the impact has been
forgotten. My Daddy
got beat for defending
his seat, still many
more like him
neglected to teach the
importance of speech
and the ways of
old when our stories
were told by the
griot around
campfires and stoves,
barbershops and hot combs.
History repeats, even
once buried beneath
the dispassionate feet
of such subsequent generations
drifting away
on the convective heat of
such turbulent days.
Leaving behind the
children of loss
to bear the cross
of the rapidly fading
memory of what we
were and are and
still can be.

TIMES THEY ARE A-CHANGIN

times, they are a-changin',
revolution is in the air
while we stand at the brink
of the kitchen sink,
frantically washing the distress
from our hair.

SOMETIMES THE WORLD DON'T MAKE NO CENTS

Sometimes the world don't make no sense.
Vertigo mauls our mind, leaves us lost,
wondering, wandering towards chaotic
events and dysfunction. Too blinded
by accusations to recognize the path
of least resistance, opportunity is
a drive by shooting. Random events,
like the birth of a quasar or
the unexpected discovery of pollution
in the most innocuous places
tend to drive all anticipation from
the heart of our concern. Too much
information can kill a man
as surely as the government,
a bureaucratic thing of emotionless,
dogmatic intent. I don't want
to be a slave to my own lack
of inner vision, but so much of what
is known is controlled by an
electronic oversight so that all life has
lost its flavor. Too much sugar
filled, tooth decay inducing sound bites
meant to placate the beast who
slumbers just beneath our perceptions
of reality, leaves us spent,
a value-less coin once meant
for circulation, cast aside,
tucked away inside a collector's case
never to see value again.

HISTORICAL ARCHAEOLOGY

Trust me, take me, talk to me about my
freedoms, god-given gifts and illusions;
previous entanglements and present
day confusions. Wish me luck as I look
through the burned out structures that crashed down
around my convictions, the lattice-works
upon which pain and hurt and love and loss
and iron crosses bear the weight of long
dead conceits and the ultimate
acceptance of triumphs and defeats.
Watch me, Watchmen, constantly vigilant.
Left alone in the dark. An unseen spark
adrift amidst the unremarkable.
Intent on illumination, I am,
unto myself, a singular
equation. Powerless against the
relentless march of mathematical
precision. Leaving me to twist and spin
along the shared space on the head
of a pin. Love me. Love me for who I
am and was and what's done. Embrace your long-
forgotten son. Devil; Angel; Damned;
Divine. Undefined.

LOST
(I never thought that I could take it this far)

Inspect me closely,
try to find the hidden seams,
the cracks that show through
to the other side of reality.
My greatest adventures
seemed to be squandered
by the prospects of my fear
for unmarked borders.
Not that I have an issue
with crossing those lines,
it's the hurt manifested in the eyes
of those left behind
that makes me regret
the passage of time.
And sometimes, the open arms
of the residents of freedom's lands
don't serve to drown out the cries
of the Protestants.

OH MY

bees and lions and
dragons and the devil
out there. far away
from the place to feel
safe and breathe in
mama's cinnamon air.
even as the world
rushes up like a quickly
rising sidewalk,
echoes in stone canyons
repeating these frantic calls
to her. Is it
a lost son who is gone,
gone away for good?
a terrible fate,
if it's too late,
to escape,
if I could.

I WANT TO GO BACK TO WRIGLEYVILLE

I want to go back to Wrigleyville,
but it is so far from what I've ever known.
I was a full grown man when I first beheld
this awesome tribute
to the imagined, the possibilities.

A downstate boy watching from afar,
left out of the new economy;
is there any wonder then,
that its beauty dulled beneath the glow
of lights and bars and parking fees?

A game for a large family
would've cost more than my father's salary.
Besides, why would he save to give to a game
that robbed his brother so long ago?

A knocked around prospect with stories
of past glory and love for a game
with a stranghold on us each,
no one else would hit, pitch or field with me;
Dr. J had begun to rule with flash
and highlights and afro-ed defiance,
painting a national pastime
with wide strokes of suburban colors
and faces that no longer looked like me
so that one by one the sandlot grew
more diminished by the conspicuous
absence of enthusiasm
and a nation-wide skew
towards a brand new austerity.

My uncle, they lied, could hit a ball,
drop his bat, pick up a glove, shag the fly

and throw himself out at home.

I tried and tried. Tossing the ball high, swinging
for the fences; Swoosh!
Ignoring the near misses.

I was Willie Stargell. Bill Madlox,
who was from my hometown. Reggie Jackson
playing for the Yankees. And then
my uncle pulled me aside, sat me down
and watched a game; "Hey! Hey!
It's unbelievable! No doubt about it!"

My love then was on its way. Wrigley
would become my Mecca, a dreamland,
calling to me, and no other team
would ever matter, even as I drove by
slowly, all these years later, and wondered
at the cost of a ticket
and lamented the loss of interest.

QUARANTINE

got us out here hustlin' for dollars
while the world breaks,
and now you wanna know what it is,
just what it takes?

while a new reality is being
sharply drawn into focus?

as kids scramble for meals,
breaking their isolation
to pick up their breakfast and
lunches from closed down
school campuses?

what this requires from you and me,
in retrospect, however,
is that we are meant to believe
that it's them, though, right?
that it's their fault that
there are literally
dragons lair's worth of loot
stashed beneath the feet of a fraction
of a percentage point's elite?

that this is what the American dream
is supposed to look like
in the midst of a quarantine?

UNTITLED

intense,
fiery consequence,
indolence;
so, who pays
when fate seeks
recompense?
no one.
we can no longer
stifle
the scream
as thrashing
black and brown
bodies demand
recognition
from
the American Dream.
but--
what does
it all mean?
when it seems
that the
presidency itself
is set in opposition
against me?
who do i trust
when the
protectors
and servers
of us
are more likely
to bust
their guns
when
i menacingly

wield
a snickers bar
and get beat
and stomped
while calling
for mom
as opposed
to being peacefully
arrested for
a black church
bombing?
or, maybe it's
simply
all in the timing.
either way,
what use is there
in praying
to the same
dude that
decided that you
would be better
served
as a third
world citizen
in a country
built upon
cotton candy
clouds that
spring and leap
just out of reach
of such
a lowly
minority as me?

THIS WORLD AIN'T MADE FOR LOVERS

This world ain't made for lovers,
for the gentle of heart, the caring,
hopeful, jubilant soul.
It's a cold, dark thing
that feeds on spite
and, by its very nature,
abhors the light of searching,
seeking beings
untethered from the stolid earth,
which stifles the imaginings
of free flying forms
aloft in blue skies
and on out across
the vastness of all
space and time.

This world fears its end.
Fears an evolution which leaves behind
the concrete that cements in place
an acceptance of dysfunction
as the norm, as opposed to
what could be,
if we were only just
allowed to let go
and dream.

You see,

dreamers tend to fall in love;
with people, with beauty,
with hope and trust and the
portent of possibilities
that resides within
each human being.

We'd remake this world,
if we were just allowed,
and find a place for each
beneath the connected,
continuous embrace
of a seldom perfect,
often tumultuous sky.

SPENT SHELLS AND SEA SHELLS

Spent shells like sea shells
strewn across cracked concrete
which stands in for the sandy beaches
on some far away, island paradise
that seems so far out of reach,
to a jump out boy who dreams
of golden gleams and live streams
and less an opportunity
and more so the means
to move about in full on
fuck you mode
as the whole world withdraws
in fear for kicking over
the wrong rock and stirring up
old memories of what
this angry soul could have been
if given the gift of recognition.
Do you see me? Can you hear me?
Well, what about the metallic ring
of hot brass raining down on asphalt
and the screams of rage
that only then begins to permeate
deep beneath the thickened, callous skin
of my fellow countrymen?
We were promised yachts,
vacation homes on sandy beaches,
or at least,
forty acres, mules and the chance
to take a shot at fulfilling
the truth of what it means
to be a part of the great
American Dream--

SUCCESS LOOMS

I stand at the brink.
Success looms like the sunrise.
Fear yet overclouds.

ABOUT THE AUTHOR

I turned 50 years old soon after a rare cosmic alignment. A Jet Black Man, I am meant to defy convention. I've always seen the strings, though, pondered at the accidental glimpses at the cracks in the curtains, the goings on behind the scenes. No wonder then that I have so comfortably retreated into solitude. So, why now, you may ask? Why chose this moment to crawl out into the open, dazed and dazzled by the neon light of this relentless reality? Well, it was my son. He made me do it. My first born, he arrived upon this plane 6 years ago and he doesn't care one frickin bit for my hesitance, for my uncertainty. He demands answers. He seeks out the Light. Not the sickly blue, paliative glow of commerce, but the Light of Reason and Understanding and Comfort and Compassion. We'll search together.
 – gzus

Thank you for supporting indie literature!

Shop more titles and learn about our outsider authors at **creativeonionpress.com**.

Power to the readers.

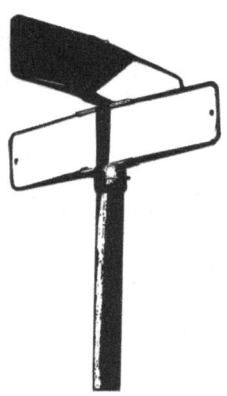

www.ingramcontent.com/pod-product-compliance
Lightning Source LLC
Chambersburg PA
CBHW011131070526
44583CB00023B/2986